Facing Cancer as a Friend

Facing Cancer as a Friend:
How to Support Someone who has Cancer
2nd Edition
Published by Connected to the Vine Publishing

All Scripture is taken from the King James Version of the Holy Bible,
Copyright © 1982 by Thomas Nelson

Cover Photo by Joshua Ness on Unsplash

Some names and identifying details have been changed to protect
the privacy of individuals.

No part of this book should be construed as medical advice.
Neither the publisher nor the author shall be held liable

Copyright © 2019 Heather Erickson
Heatherericksonauthor.com
heatherericksonauthor@gmail.com

All rights reserved.
No part of this book may be reproduced in any form without permission in
writing from the publisher,
except in the case of brief quotations.

Published in the United States by Connected to the Vine Publishing,
554 98th Avenue NE, Minneapolis, Minnesota, 55434.
ISBN: 9781087047423

Facing Cancer as a Friend

How to Support Someone who has Cancer

By Heather Erickson

For my amazing husband, Dan,
And my beautiful daughters,
Summer, Samantha, and Emily

Contents

Foreword	11
Introduction	13
The Smith Family	15
Diagnosis...Cancer	17
Unsolicited Advice	19
A Spiritual Problem	23
Apples and Oranges	27
Denial	31
A Friend in Need	33
Be Prepared	37
The Ring Theory	39
Visits, Notes, and Calls	47

What NOT To Say to Someone Who Has Cancer	57
Helpful Things You CAN Say	65
Doing Something Helpful	69
Special Skills You May Have	77
Bringing Meals	81
Gifts	89
A Chemo Day Bag	93
Caregivers and Children	97
When Your Friend Has Died	107
Afterword	113
Acknowledgments	115
Other Books in the *Facing Cancer* Series	117

Foreword

"You have cancer." I'll never forget the day I heard those chilling words that most everyone fears. Life as we knew it changed that day and has never been the same since. It has now been three and a half years since hearing those words, and it has been a continuous battle for my life. During that time, my wife, Heather and I have become experts at something we never wanted anything to do with. We've learned the hard way, what's helpful and what isn't.

Today, most people with cancer don't have to stay in hospital. Advances in outpatient treatment and symptom management allow patients to remain at home. During this time help and encouragement from non-professional friends and family is crucial. Our friends and family have been invaluable, helping to lift the burden of cancer when we've needed it the most.

Many studies have found that cancer survivors who have strong emotional support tend to adjust better to the changes cancer brings to their lives. They have a more positive outlook, often report better quality of life, and sometimes a longer life. Research has shown that people with cancer need caring friends, and we sure do. You can make a big difference in the life of someone with cancer or any other major, life-altering diagnosis.

My wife Heather has been my faithful caregiver during these tough times, and I can't recommend her enough as an authority on helping those fighting cancer or any physical challenge.

Facing Cancer as a Friend will address ways that you can support people as they "walk through the valley of the shadow of death." Heather will give you practical ways to help the people in your life facing cancer, whether a family member, friend or someone you barely know.

Many of the ideas in this book are simple. Some may seem counter-intuitive and will stretch you. Others will require you to have a certain amount of faith. With the help of *Facing Cancer as a Friend*, you will be more equipped to lovingly support your friend or family member through what may be the lowest point of their life.

Dan Erickson was diagnosed with stage IV lung cancer in 2012. He was the pastor of a small community church at the time of his diagnosis. He was also a real estate agent for twenty-two years. He has six children; three of them were still school-aged and living at home. After his diagnosis, he wrote and published two books: The ABC's of the Bible: 200 Two-Minute lessons on the Basics of the Bible, and Praying the Psalms: a Handbook to Intimacy with God. He went home to the Lord on April 26, 2019.

We miss him greatly.

Introduction

So many people would like to help their friends through their cancer journey, but they aren't sure how—and for good reason. Cancer is a frightening diagnosis and we often feel powerless to combat its effects.

The good news is that even though cancer is devastating, patients and their families can still live fulfilling lives after diagnosis, during treatment, and beyond. Supportive family and friends play a huge part in this.

In this revised and updated version of *Facing Cancer as a Friend*, you'll find a wealth of ideas for how to help the people in your life who have cancer. As you read the suggestions in this book, you'll be surprised by some things. You'll also find yourself saying, "I could do that!"

You will also find a chapter that includes 3 pieces of advice for helping widows/widowers and their children after a loved one has died.

For more great information on living with cancer and supporting those who are, check out my website: *facingcancerwithgrace.com*. You will find many resources, both in my blog posts and on my resource pages.

Anytime you wish to contact me, feel free to send an email to *heatherericksonauthor@gmail.com*. I'd love to know more about your story and the concerns and questions you have.

~Heather Erickson

The Smith Family

To illustrate the purpose of this book, I would like to share with you the story of the Smith family. It's important to remember that no two people have the same exact experience with their disease and its treatment. The responses in the Smith family's story are a few of the more common reactions that people facing cancer get from friends, family, and even strangers. Let's take a look at them to examine why someone would respond that way, and why it can cause distress for a cancer patient and their family. This story highlights why knowing what to say and do (as well as what not to) can make a big difference in the lives of patients, their caregivers, and children.

The Smith Family: Diagnosis...Cancer

Martha Smith had been losing weight—a lot of it. She had no appetite and she'd been training for a marathon, so it didn't alarm her. But then the fatigue set in and one day she woke up and felt too tired to get out of bed.

When her husband Greg came home from work that evening, she was still there, yellow with jaundice. He rushed Martha to the hospital where the doctor ordered a battery of tests. Martha had stage IV pancreatic cancer.

How could she have cancer? She'd always lived a healthy lifestyle. She was still so young. They had children at home. How would Greg take care of their children alone, while Martha was sick—or worse—if she died? All these things swam through their minds as they asked the doctor about her chance of survival.

The doctor's tone was somber. His face showed little emotion as he explained the situation, balancing hope with the grave reality of Martha's situation. "Even though we are treating the cancer," said the doctor, "You will need to begin preparing yourselves and your children. Your time is limited."

Because her cancer had metastasized, she had a prognosis of three to six months to live if it was left untreated. Eighty percent of all pancreatic cancer patients die within a year of diagnosis. For stage IV patients, the picture is even grimmer.

Martha's treatment options were limited, but it was possible that with the right treatment, her life could be extended. The oncologist presented options ranging from palliative (comfort) care to aggressive treatment. Somewhere in between, was a combination of traditional chemotherapy combined with a targeted treatment. The targeted treatment would go after the specific cancer cells while sparing the healthy cells. This combination was known to increase survival by an average of nearly six months.

Martha and Greg looked at one another. Six months. It seemed so short. Yet, in the face of death, six months was more precious than gold. Martha and Greg were especially concerned about their kids. They had three daughters and a son, aged seven to seventeen. They needed time.

"I would like to do the combination treatment," Martha said, trying to hold back her tears. Greg squeezed her hand reassuringly. They could hardly believe they were having this conversation. In the following weeks, as they told family and friends about Martha's diagnosis, the Smiths were taken aback by the reactions they received.

The Smith Family: Unsolicited Advice

Greg asked his boss if he could cut back on his hours at work. He wanted to be able to go to Martha's appointments with her. He also wanted to take care of things around the house that Martha usually handled, because the doctor said that Martha would likely experience intense fatigue during treatment. By the end of the day, word spread throughout the whole office.

Greg was heading toward his car when Charlie, from the mailroom, approached, waving a piece of paper in the air. "I heard about Martha. I needed to share this with you." Charlie handed Greg the paper. "*Big Pharma* doesn't want people to know about this, but it's out there. Martha doesn't need to die."

Greg read several paragraphs, each about a person whose cancer had been "cured" by canned asparagus. "Just two tablespoons a day will do it." Greg looked at Charlie who seemed proud of his discovery. Greg wasn't sure what to say. Greg had been studying up on how cancer functioned. He knew that two tablespoons of canned asparagus weren't going to take care of the ravaging beast in Martha's body. As he read more from the essay Charlie had given him, Greg noticed that several of the people who claimed the asparagus had cured them were also using some form of traditional treatment, such as chemo or radiation. "And yet," he thought, "canned asparagus gets the credit." Still, he didn't want to get into an argument with Charlie, so he thanked him as he climbed into his car to go home.

When people give cancer patients unsolicited advice, it's often in the form of a promised cure, such as an oil, a supplement, or in this case, canned asparagus. If you think this is far-fetched, I can assure you, it isn't. By the time we gave up keeping track, we had been told about more than fifty unique cures—and one of them was canned asparagus. Many of them were repeated by different people. They all thought they knew the secret that would solve our problem.

Behind this is a desire to help, without knowing how to. While Charlie was conspiracy-minded, his heart was in the right place. He had heard about something that he thought might help Greg's wife, so he shared it. He'd essentially become an evangelist for the anti-pharmaceutical movement. Charlie's not alone. More than 27% of Americans believe that *Big Pharma* has a cure for cancer, but is suppressing it so that they can continue to make money on treatments they sell.

It isn't my intention to be the pharmaceutical industry's representative or defender. My goal is to help patients and their families advocate for themselves. This includes explaining why the demonization of the pharmaceutical industry and the medical community as a whole, often hurts patients and their families.

The decisions that Martha and Greg made were being called into question at a time when they already felt insecure about many things, not the least of which was Martha's very survival.

On the surface so-called cures and quick-fix answers slander drug companies and the doctors. But when you look deeper, they do something far more damaging. They question the judgment of the patient, their caregiver, and their family.

Even worse, they can cause divisions in families that haven't come to a consensus regarding treatment choices. They also cause patients to try unproven remedies rather than tested and statistically reliable methods of fighting the patient's specific form of cancer. This wastes precious time and a patient who may have been curable when they were first diagnosed can end up losing their life because cancer spread while they were eating asparagus rather than going through medically supervised treatment.

I know of one family in which the elderly patient felt such pressure by her daughter to use a "natural cure" rather than follow her doctor's advice that she gave in to keep the peace. At first, she seemed to be doing fine. Her daughter began to blog about how well her mom was doing on her new cancer diet. But after a few months, cancer began to spread rapidly. By that point, the doctors could only offer comfort care and she died very quickly.

Did you notice that Charlie never asked how Martha was doing, or how Greg and the kids were holding up? So often, the people who advocate a diet or cure don't ask questions of any sort. They're too busy telling people what to do. They also rarely offer any help beyond the link to a web page touting some cure to buy.

Cancer cure evangelists like Charlie can be very persistent. Unfortunately, this can lead the patient and caregiver to avoid these friends completely, because they don't want to feel the pressure, or have yet another awkward conversation. This is very sad, indeed.

The Smith Family: A Spiritual Problem

As Sunday church service was letting out, Ellen, one of the choir members, stopped Martha in the hallway. "You have been weighing heavily on my heart ever since I heard. I was watching a video online last night posted by a man gifted in the prophetic. He said that cancer is caused by unforgiveness. I just knew that God meant for me to tell you that."

Martha arched her eyebrows, drew in a breath and mentally counted to ten. This was a coping mechanism she developed early on in parenthood.

Ellen continued. "He said that in order to be healed, you need to fast. No food—and only water to drink. Do this for seven days. Also, you need to pray for everyone in your life who's ever wronged you. Then God will heal you."

"I can't even think of anyone who's wronged me." Martha paused a moment, considering whether there was anything to what Ellen was telling her. "I've been hurt a time or two, but I forgave them long ago."

"Are you sure?" asked Ellen.

Martha could see that Ellen didn't believe her. What if Martha had anger toward someone and just didn't realize it?

She knew that bitterness was bad for your health, but could it actually cause cancer? She asked Greg what he thought. "Ellen thinks there's someone I haven't forgiven." Greg scoffed. Martha never held anything against anyone. In Greg's opinion, she was a little too forgiving.

Martha told him that she was supposed to fast as well. Could she really be considering this? Greg was afraid Martha might take what Ellen had said to heart. She was already fifteen pounds underweight. They'd seen a nutritionist at the cancer center who put Martha on a high protein diet. She said that 20% of cancer patient deaths are results of malnutrition. And Ellen is advocating that Martha fast?

Later that night, Ellen called their house. When Greg answered, she told him that it was very important that Martha not take chemotherapy. "She needs to place her trust in God for her healing. If she does treatment, then she doesn't have faith; and God won't heal her."

Greg was stunned. Ellen and Martha had been good friends for many years. Their families spent a lot of time together. Ellen knew that Martha was a woman who placed great faith in Jesus. How could she say such a thing? He shook off the shock he was feeling and mustered his strength. "Martha is relying on God. She knows that everything she has comes from Him. He gives her the very air she breathes."

There was a hush on Ellen's side of the phone line. Greg wondered if she'd hung up for a minute. Then he heard her exhale as if she'd been holding her breath.

He continued. He was on a roll. "When we sit down at the table for dinner, we pray, giving thanks to God for the food that we eat. That being said, is it lacking faith to have a job in order to pay for that food? Is it lacking faith when we cook the food in order to make the meal? Would having true faith require us to sit down, expecting the meal to appear before us miraculously?"

"Of course not," said Ellen, softly.

"Then why do you expect our health and healing to happen with no effort at all on our part?

Ellen didn't have an answer. She soon hung up after a clumsy apology. Greg felt embarrassed. Was he too hard on her? She meant well.

The Smith family derived much strength and comfort from their faith. Unfortunately, the negative responses from some members of their faith community have been hurtful. Ellen was just one example. She had long been a good friend to Martha and Greg, but when they needed her support most, she gave them what amounted to spiritual abuse. Ellen didn't realize that questioning a cancer patient's faith because of their decision to receive traditional treatment is hurtful.

Likewise, it's painful when someone tells a patient that they are sick as a result of sin, such as holding a grudge against someone. While sin can cause all sorts of problems in a person's life, the presence of illness is not necessarily the result of sin. There are many books on logic and reasoning that you can read if you would like to go into that more in-depth. Instead, let's move on to another spiritual issue: Fasting.

Fasting is a spiritual discipline practiced in many faith traditions. It has numerous spiritual benefits, and for a healthy person, fasting can also have physical benefits. For someone who is ill, however, fasting can be deadly.

Cancer rapidly eats away at muscle tissue. For that reason, eating a diet high in protein is often advocated by oncology nutritionists. As Greg had learned, twenty percent of the deaths in cancer patients is a result of malnutrition. Fasting would certainly speed this process up.

Faith is a sensitive topic. It is extremely important to people. The problem with using a person's faith to pressure them into making (often poor) health care choices is that it can push them to make choices they otherwise never would. It can also cause emotional distress at a time when they really don't need any added burden.

When our family experienced this, I felt very angry. My husband's life was at stake. The amount of time we had left together, and the quality of that time, depended a great deal on the decisions that we made. The people pressuring him to stop chemotherapy treatment wouldn't be living with the results of that decision. We would.

The Smith Family: Apples and Oranges

The next day, Greg and Martha's son, Nick, came home from school in tears. Greg had to coax what happened out of him. After a scoop of ice cream in the back yard, Nick admitted to his dad that his sixth-grade teacher had pulled him aside that day to tell him how sorry she was that his mom was going to die. "She told me that it's a horrible way to go."

"Why would she say such a thing?" asked Greg.

Nick sniffed. "She told me her aunt died of it ten years ago. She said she'll never forget the agony her aunt was in."

"The nerve of her," Greg steamed. "What right did she have to say that?"

"She told me that when Mom dies if I needed to talk, I could go to her," said Nick.

Sabrina, Nick's younger sister, overheard their conversation. "Mommy's going to be okay," she assured them. "April was here today." April was Martha's best friend. "She said Mommy will be fine. April had cancer eight years ago and she's fine."

"Honey," Greg put his hand on Sabrina's shoulder. "April had a different kind of cancer. Thankfully, they found it very early and were able to operate and treat her with almost no chance of it coming back." He didn't want to shatter his daughter's optimism, but he and Martha also felt very strongly that they should be honest with their children. "Mom's cancer is different."

Their kids didn't need the details that Nick's teacher had shared, but they also didn't need to be misled by Martha's friend, Amy. They had to know that this was going to be difficult so that they could emotionally prepare for what was about to happen in their family.

Martha put her face in her hands and began to sob. It had only been 2 weeks since they'd begun to tell people about her cancer, and everyone seemed to have some point of view that they needed to assert. Yet, only a few people had offered to pray for them or bring a meal.

This illustrated a couple of things. The first is the problem of comparing situations. Comparisons are never helpful in relationships, no matter what you are looking at. Comparing cancers is unfair, and unproductive. Each patient deserves to have their own unique experience. Their cancer journey will be unlike anyone else's. That's because they aren't like anyone else. We're all individuals. Some cancer journeys are long and others are short. Some cancers are healed and others aren't. All cancer journeys are frightening.

Obviously, Nick's teacher had a very painful experience with her aunt's death from cancer. What happened to her aunt is not necessarily the same experience that Martha will have. Nick's teacher was momentarily reliving a frightening time in her life. Projecting those fears onto Nick and his family was wrong. Even if she had been talking to

Greg, who is an adult, rather than Nick, she should have kept her thoughts regarding her aunt's death to herself.

April was Martha's best friend. She had been a cancer patient herself and thinking of Martha going through cancer was difficult for her. She wished she could wave a magic wand and have it all go away. She wanted to encourage her friend and her friend's children.

So, she did the opposite of what Nick's teacher did. She compared her cancer experience to Martha's, but because her cancer was very treatable, she couldn't relate to the idea of knowing that in all likelihood she would die. This response can make a cancer patient feel very alone. Martha was reminded that even her best friend didn't understand how serious the situation was. You can't brush off a cancer diagnosis like a skinned knee. Doing so belittles the patient and his or her concerns and fears.

The other issue here is the confusion her comments caused for Greg and Martha's children. What April said didn't line up with what Sabrina's parents had told her. Nick's teacher didn't help, either. As a child, Nick was likely already very afraid of what would happen as a result of his mom's cancer. Between April's comments and those of Nick's teacher, the water was getting pretty muddy.

People outside of the family should never share their own thoughts, opinions, or fears with a patient's child. Always respect the parents' wishes and decisions regarding their children.

The Smith Family: Denial

Martha and Greg had felt good about the plan of action they'd decided on with Martha's doctor. But now, everything seemed muddled and Martha began to doubt their decision. She didn't have time to experiment with other options. What if she'd made the wrong choice?

"I'm just trying to buy time," she said to her dad on the phone that night. "I need to get things in order and spend what life I have left with Greg and the kids."

"Don't think that way," said her dad. "You have to think positive. How's Nick doing in baseball? Did he have another good game?" He changed the subject and avoided conversations with her from that point on. That way he didn't need to think about losing her.

Martha's dad spent his entire life dealing with problems the same way. He avoided them. He didn't like to think about things that were frightening or that he didn't understand. Martha's cancer was no different.

I will never tell a parent how they should (or shouldn't) respond to their son or daughter's cancer. As a parent, what you are facing is unthinkable. You will grieve in your own way, at your own pace. However, Martha's dad can teach us something. How we have dealt with stressful situations in our past will likely be how we deal with a loved one's cancer diagnosis. One of the best things you can do before responding to your friend is to consider whether your response is a healthy one.

Have people ever said that you're overbearing, that you don't take people's feelings seriously, or that you avoid them altogether? Take a good honest look at yourself, your fears, and your agendas. When you have a friend or relative staring death in the face, you need to push all of that aside and be there for them on their terms.

The Smith Family: A Friend in Need

Three days after Martha's first chemotherapy treatment, Greg was at work when he got a phone call from Erin, their neighbor. The Smith's dog Trixie, had once again dug under the fence and escaped. Lately, she hadn't been getting as much attention, so out of boredom, she thought she'd make her own fun. Greg cringed, anticipating a lecture on the leash laws.

Erin surprised him when she said, "I only wanted you to know that she is safe. By the way, I heard about Martha. I'm so sorry."

"Thank you," said Greg. He wondered how she heard. He and Martha hardly knew their neighbors. A twinge of guilt hit him.

"You have a lot to deal with right now. Would it help if I took Trixie for a walk each morning to run off some of her energy?" Erin asked. "It would give me an excuse to get some exercise, myself."

Greg was stunned. "Oh, you don't have to do that."

"I'd like to," Erin assured him. "Just leave her in your yard when you head off to work, or when you get up on the days you stay home. I'll take her for a walk. When I'm done, I'll put her back in your yard so Martha doesn't need to answer the door if she's resting."

"Wow. I don't know what to say."

"Think nothing of it. Oh, and give Martha my number in case she needs anything while you're at work. I'm always at home. She can call any time."

"Thank you," said Greg. "That means a lot."

"You are all in my prayers."

Late that summer, when the vegetables in Erin's garden were ready to harvest, she packed up a basket for the Smith family every few days so they would have fresh vegetables. She said she had more than she could ever eat. And once a week she would make a big pot of soup, keeping a couple of servings out for herself. Soon the Smiths insisted that she join them for dinner. The neighbors who were once strangers divided by a picket fence were now good friends united in some strange way by Martha's cancer.

Why You Matter

The way you respond to your friend's cancer can either lift their burden or add to it. By showing them love and compassion, you are doing more than taking care of a physical need. You are helping to bolster their confidence that there are good people in the world. It can make their situation look less hopeless.

By the third century, BCE Quintus Ennius wrote,

"Amicus certus in re incerta cernitur."

Translated from the Latin this means, "A sure friend is known when in difficulty." This is likely where we get the proverb, "A friend in need is a friend indeed."

In the 16th century, the proverb was recorded in John Heywood's *A Dialogue Conteynyng Prouerbes and Epigrammes*, 1562.

> "Prove [that is, test] thy friend ere [before] thou have need; but, in-deed
> A friend is never known till a man have need.
> Before I had need, my most present foes
> Seemed my most friends; but thus the world goes."

Most cancer patients and caregivers I have known have remarked something similar to Heywood's sentiments. They grieve the friends they thought would be there for them but weren't. At the same time, they are in awe of the people who have stood by them in their time of trial, often people they hardly knew prior to facing cancer.

Not only are friends like this uplifting, but they are also inspiring. They teach us how to be better friends so that when this cancer journey is over, and we regain our strength, we can be there for people who face difficulties.

The Smith family's story is not unusual. On the contrary, it is the common experience of families facing cancer. Thankfully, you can be an uncommonly good friend. The fact that you're reading this book attests to that.

36

Be Prepared

Our Story

When my husband was diagnosed with stage IV lung cancer in 2012, we received a wide spectrum of responses from family and friends. Some people, with good intentions, caused us a lot of pain. Others supported us and made an amazing difference in our ability to cope.

Since you're reading this, I am sure that you want to help the people in your life who are going through the fire of cancer or some other life-altering diagnosis. You have unique strengths and gifts that can benefit them at the point of their greatest need. I want to help you know how to use these abilities to their maximum potential. Helping someone in their time of need doesn't have to feel like a burden. In fact, it should bless you as much as your friend.

Learning that a friend has cancer can be a shock. It's difficult news to hear. Take time to acknowledge and cope with your own emotions about the diagnosis before you see him or her. This way, you can keep the focus on your friend.

Keep in mind that the way you would deal with cancer may not be the way your friend will choose to deal with it. This has been known to cause conflict in relationships and stress for the patient and their family at a time when they don't need it. One thing that can help avoid any problems like these is the Ring Theory.

Be Prepared: The Ring Theory

The Ring Theory was created by breast cancer survivor and clinical psychologist Dr. Susan Silk Ph.D., and arbitrator/mediator, Barry Goldman. The gist of it is this: Comfort in. Dump out.

The Patient
Take out a piece of paper. You are going to make something that looks like a target. In the middle of the page, draw a small circle about the size of a quarter. This is the bullseye. Label it with the patient's name. The patient is in the center because the patient is the center of their cancer universe. It is everyone else's job to support them. No one is allowed to dump on the patient. For example, no one should talk about the ways that the patient's cancer is hurting or burdening them. This would only make the patient feel bad—even guilty.

When Karen, a breast cancer patient, was no longer able to bring meals to neighborhood functions or help with the kids' school activities, a few people remarked at how hard it was without her, since they depended on her. Some people say things like this to let the patient know they are important and missed. However, this added a new layer of guilt to Karen's shoulders, even though that was never her friends' intentions. So don't say anything to the patient regarding the effects of his/her cancer on you. Instead, listen to and comfort the patient. It's about them—not you.

Spouse/Caregiver

To make the next level in your "target," draw another circle around the "patient" circle. That's the "spouse/caregiver" ring. They're next in line for support. The only person who can complain or "dump" on the caregiver is the patient, and they will likely be doing plenty of this. Everyone else should listen to and comfort the spouse or caregiver. They are enduring a lot right now, so they need all the support they can get.

Immediate Family

Next, make the target even larger by drawing a third circle around the spouse/caregiver circle (which is around the patient circle). This will represent the immediate family. Immediate family can vent to anyone other than the patient and the spouse/caregiver. Immediate family members can also dump on one another. They all share the same concerns and are able to comfort one another in a unique and special way.

Other People

Draw a fourth circle around the immediate family circle. This one represents extended family and close friends. This group of people can be an incredible source of support to people in the smaller target rings. Often they provide strength to immediate family members who feel like falling apart.

A fifth circle will represent colleagues and acquaintances such as fellow club members or people from church. Each subsequent circle of people is a little more distant from the patient and their situation.

Lookie-Loos

On the outer edge of the rings is a group of people called the lookie-loos. These are people who have nothing at stake. They are the grocer or the guy that visits your garage sale, someone from church who hasn't spoken to the patient or caregiver in months or someone who happened to come upon the patient or caregiver's blog. lookie-loos aren't allowed to dump on anyone, but they can offer comfort. In fact, many times a lookie-loo has been a great source of encouragement to our family.

Rule of Thumb

Dumping or venting is anything that isn't solely and directly supportive. Never dump on someone in a circle closer to the patient than the circle you're in. For example, a friend would not dump on a patient's parent or spouse. But they could talk to another friend or someone outside of the situation.

Knowing which circle you occupy in relation to the patient, requires some self-awareness. It's important to note that this way of categorizing which ring you are in, in no way indicates how important you are to the patient and/or caregiver, or how important they are to you. It's simply a way of showing restraint in consideration of others.

Hopefully, this explains, in a nutshell, the etiquette of who to comfort (anyone who is hurting) and who to dump on (only people in a circle larger than yours—and never the patient). Remember the adage, "It's not about me". While it may affect you, dumping on anyone in a circle closer to the patient than you are can be seen as insensitive, selfish, and tacky, even when said with the best of intentions. By the way, this works for any crisis someone may go through; health, financial, marital, etc.

You can also find an image of this on my website at: *http://facingcancerwithgrace.com/circle-of-support/*

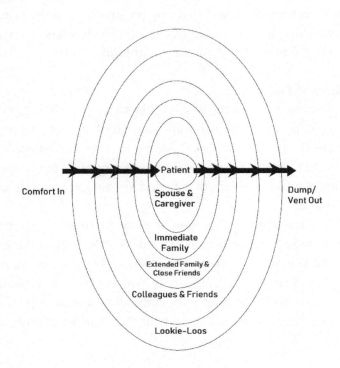

Follow the Golden Rule

People are often uncomfortable around people who have cancer, even if they've been friends for a long time. They aren't sure of what to say—and what not to say. A lot of the time it's because they worry about making the patient feel embarrassed or sad. This is especially difficult for people who have never had a serious illness in their family.

Jesus said, "Do unto others as you would have them do unto you." His words can really help when deciding how to treat a friend who has cancer, or their spouse/caregiver. How would you want to be treated if you were in their shoes? That being said...

Think about your friend's point of view. Understand that they may not react to a given situation the same way you would. How do they typically react to difficult trials? Do they withdraw? Or do they want to talk? If you aren't sure of what they want, just ask. The key here is respect. Honor their feelings and decisions.

Although each person with cancer is different, there are some general guidelines.

Is Your Friend Up To Visiting?

Make sure your friend is feeling up to visiting before you arrive. Let them know you understand if they'd rather postpone until a more convenient time. If they choose to wait a few days (or even a few weeks) before getting together with you, don't take it personally. Sometimes that's just how it is with cancer. It's actually a compliment to you that they can be honest about how things are going. It shows they trust you. Later when they are feeling better, you can redeem the rain check. In the meantime, send them cards or emails to let them know you haven't forgotten them.

Be Real

That includes being humorous and fun when appropriate. A light conversation or a funny story can make a friend's day. But, don't ignore uncomfortable topics or feelings. It's important to be able to express sadness, as well. Your friend may need to talk to someone they trust. If that person is you, you should be honored.

Treat Them as You Always Have

Try not to let your friend's condition get in the way of your friendship. Ask about interests, hobbies, life events, and other topics not related to cancer. People going through treatment sometimes need a break from talking about the disease. This doesn't mean ignoring the elephant in the room. Be cheerful when you naturally would be and allow for sadness when it's appropriate.

Read His or Her Story

Do they have a blog, a social media page, group email, or another way they share their experiences with friends and family? By following their story, you are showing your friend that you care. Stay current with these updates so that your friend doesn't have to repeat experiences or information more than necessary. These updates can also be a great way to start a conversation.

A Word of Warning Considering Advice

No matter how close you are to the patient or caregiver; do not give them unsolicited advice. Just because they are sharing their concerns doesn't mean they want your advice. Don't forget the Smith Family and their well-meaning friends.

Visits, Notes, and Calls

"Come, you blessed of My Father, inherit the kingdom prepared for you from the foundation of the world: for I was hungry and you gave Me food; I was thirsty and you gave Me drink; I was a stranger and you took Me in; I was naked and you clothed Me; I was sick and you visited Me; I was in prison and you came to Me."
~Matthew 25: 34b-36

When we find out a friend is sick, our gut instinct too often is to give them space—a lot of space. We don't want to be a bother. While you need to be sensitive to your friend's need for rest, it is important that you *do* visit and call.

When someone has cancer, it is easy for them to become isolated and withdrawn for several reasons. Treatments can leave patients feeling drained of energy.

They may be immune suppressed and/or in pain, so they often stay home far more than they used to. Insensitive reactions to their illness by people they encounter out and about can also lead to feelings of loneliness and depression.

Countless studies have shown that cancer patients with strong social networks live longer and have higher survival rates, while their isolated counterparts skip more meals and often miss important appointments and prescriptions.

That's why it's important that they maintain the connection you have with your friends who are facing cancer. You can make a big impact on their quality of life. It can also help you to see for yourself if there is something more the family needs, but isn't asking for.

Anna

Years ago, my husband attended a breakfast for the men at our church. That morning he met a man named George, whose wife, Anna, had multiple sclerosis. George had been asking at his church if there was a woman who would visit the nursing home where Anna lived and read the Bible to her on occasion. So far, no one had.

When Dan came home and told me this, I considered visiting her weekly. I called Anna's husband and taking into account my schedule, her family members' visits, and the care center's schedule (meals, activities, etc.), we figured out the best day and time for a visit.

I wasn't prepared for the experience. When I walked into her room and saw a beautiful woman, much younger, and far more affected by her illness than I'd anticipated, it really shook me up. Thankfully, I was able to hold it together as I introduced myself and then read to her.

I left after an hour. Rather than going home, I drove to our church, crying the whole way. We had a pastor who specialized in visiting the homebound. Wondering how he could do this every day, I went to him in tears saying that I wanted to continue visiting Anna, but I didn't think I was cut out for it.

He told me that it wouldn't be as difficult to visit Anna in the future because I would never be as unprepared as I'd been that day. He also encouraged me to learn about multiple sclerosis in order to better understand what she felt. This raised my level of empathy and lowered any anxiety I felt about her condition.

From then on, I prayed for Anna and for our time together while I drove to the care center.

Anna's husband had asked me to read her the Bible, but I wondered if there was anything else she wanted to do, as well. When I asked her, she said that the Bible reading was what she wanted most. She told me which books of the Bible were her favorite, so I could read those, specifically. On nice sunny days, I would bring her out onto the care center's patio for some fresh air.

Once in a while, Anna would have a bad day. It was difficult to see her hurting, but I took solace in the fact that when I was there, she didn't have to hurt alone. Over the course of the next two years, I came to know Anna well. She was funny and wonderful. Eventually, a treasured friendship grew between us.

During Visits

- When visiting, remember the cardinal rule: Ask permission. Ask if it's okay to visit, where they would like you to sit, and what they feel like discussing, etc.

- Always call or text before your scheduled visit, to make sure that your friend is still feeling up for a visit. If your friend can't see you at that time, let them know it's okay and that you will reschedule when it works better for them.

- Most cancer treatments cause fatigue, so it can be difficult for patients to converse for an extended period of time. Having multiple people included in the visit will magnify this difficulty. Be sensitive to this and keep visits one on one when possible.

- Schedule visits for times other than weekends or holidays when others may visit unless of course, they have no one else. Too many visitors in a day can be tiring for patients and caregivers.

- Set a time limit for visits and phone calls, before you begin. That way you won't wear your friend out. When in doubt, stick to ten or fifteen minutes. You'll be surprised at what a day-brightener fifteen minutes can be to a cancer patient.

- If you or someone in your family becomes ill, stay clear of the patient and his/her family. Cancer treatments can lower a patient's immune system, making them more likely to get sick. It will be difficult for them to fight the bug if they do. Because of this, the patient's family also needs to avoid getting sick.

- Find out if they are in any pain or discomfort. Is there anything you can do to ease the discomfort, for example, by using pillows or moving furniture? When talking, sit or stand directly in front of your friend so they don't need to turn their head in order to talk to you, since this can bring on a wave of nausea.

- If you meet your friend at a social gathering, where the crowd is mostly standing, look for a place to sit down. It's easy to take healthy feet for granted. Along with fatigue, patients may suffer from neuropathy and other debilitating issues that make standing for long periods of time unbearable.

Our Story

Several times over the years, our kids made plans, and later had to cancel after one of their friends came down with a virus. This was always a letdown for all of the kids, but if ours caught the bug and brought it home, it would have put my husband at risk. When one of our family members did become ill, they would be quarantined in their bedroom for days to prevent the virus from spreading. It's important for friends to be honest about whether they have illness in their home, prior to visiting. As disappointing as it is to have to cancel plans, they can always be rescheduled. It is far better to be safe than to regret it later.

Keeping Up Appearances

Be prepared for changes in your friend's appearance. Weight fluctuations, hair loss, fatigue, and other symptoms such as a cough or shortness of breath are common side effects of cancer and many treatments. Yet, these side effects aren't always a part of living with cancer. Newer treatments have fewer appearance-altering side effects. You are also probably seeing your friend when they're feeling their best. Even if your friend doesn't look sick, it doesn't diminish the seriousness of what they are going through. There's a battle being waged within their body it is affecting every aspect of their life.

Regardless of how your friend looks on the outside, start your visit by saying, "It's good to see you," rather than commenting on any physical changes. It's far more polite and will reduce your chances of inadvertently hurting their feelings.

Fatigue

Even if your friend does look good, they may still tire easily. Have a heightened awareness of your friend's condition during the visit, keeping in mind that cancer patients need to manage energy for the entire day—not just during the time they have visitors. Take care that you don't leave them feeling worn out.

Many patients worry they'll offend you if they tell you they're tired. Assure your friend that you understand how taxing conversation can be and that you would like them to tell you when they start to feel tired. Also, watch for signs of fatigue, such as yawning, nodding off, rubbing eyes, and slurred speech. There are also more subtle indications such as turning pale, not maintaining eye contact, engaging less in the conversation, shifting in their seat, stretching their neck, or rolling their shoulders due to stiffness.

What if your friend is too ill to talk?

You can still visit them with them. Your presence, alone, will likely be a great comfort. While your friend might not feel like talking, they may not like being alone either. If you live close to your friend, consider shorter (15 minutes), more frequent visits.

If you live far enough away that shorter, more frequent visits aren't practical, consider a longer visit that is less intense. Bring a DVD to share with your friend. Watching a movie can be enjoyable, and the patient can rest at the same time. If you are in town for more than a day, another option is to visit in the morning for a short time, then give them a break and return later that day or the next.

Respite

Scheduling a respite visit gives physical and emotional support for the caregiver. This can be valuable for staving off caregiver burnout, especially when the patient is unable to be left alone for any length of time. Arrange to stay with your friend at a time when the caregiver can do something to take care of their own needs. This could be a couple of hours, or even a day or two. You can do some light housework while your friend rests. Not only will you be providing a practical service, but you'll also be nearby when they wake up and are ready to visit.

Read to your friend.

Give them some options and read what they like. It could be a newspaper, magazine, fiction, non-fiction or the Bible. Whatever it is, choose something that your friend won't need to concentrate on, such as a book they've read before. Then your friend can drift in and out of sleep, feeling comforted, rather than frustrated.

Hospital Visits

If you're visiting your friend in the hospital, bring needlework, a crossword puzzle, a book, or an e-reader and continue to keep your friend company even if they doze off for a few moments. Sometimes having someone there can bring a feeling of security, making it easier for the patient to rest.

As You Say Goodbye

Refer to your next visit so your friend can look forward to it. Then make sure to write it down in your planner or calendar. It's too easy for time to pass without visiting, letting opportunities fall by the wayside.

If you know the patient well and you are both comfortable with physical affection, end your visit with a hug. This isn't just encouraging, it's also very healing. Hugs release the hormone oxytocin, which makes us feel good. Hugs have been proven to lower blood pressure. They also alleviate fears, which is why children often hug objects such as teddy bears when they're afraid. Hugs lower your heart rate and reduce cortisol, the stress hormone. And, they help our bodies release tension and send calming messages to the brain.

What if your friend is too ill to visit?

Whether you choose to call, text, send a note or email will depend a lot on how your friend is doing. If your friend is up to it, phone calls from friends and family are a welcomed distraction. There are few things as comforting as the voice of a friend or loved one.

If your friend is very ill, rather than long, infrequent calls, make short calls at regular intervals. Ask what times are best for you to call. If they call you, try to return their messages right away when you know that they are awake and ready to talk. Some types of cancer treatments and symptoms can make talking painful or difficult. These include radiation, mouth sores, and breathlessness, among others. Just ask your friend if they are comfortable talking for a few minutes to catch up.

If it's painful to talk, text messaging, emails, and cards are a great way to remind your friend that you still care for your friend despite changes in what they can do or how they look. When you send notes, cards, and emails, let your friend know it's okay if he or she doesn't reply. If you end the note with, "I'll be in touch soon," be sure to follow through. It can help to write a reminder in your appointment book so you don't forget.

If they can converse comfortably, ask questions. This will help them feel heard and allow them an opportunity to process what is happening by sharing their thoughts with you. Remember, it's always better to listen more than you speak.

Phone Fatigue

Because the very act of conversing can be fatiguing, limit the time you spend with your friend on the phone. When in doubt, stick to under ten minutes.

Just getting a phone call can interfere with times of rest. A 2015 Bank of America *Trends in Consumer Mobility Report* found that 71% of people over the age of 18 usually sleep with or next to their mobile phone—and 3% of those people said they sleep with their device in their hand. This goes to show that people have a hard time taking a break from their phones.

It can be especially difficult for patients to turn the phone off since they're often waiting for calls from their medical team. This doesn't mean that you shouldn't call your friend. It is just a note of caution to be aware that when you call, your friend may answer even if they're resting. That's okay. You don't have a magic ball. Just ask right away, "Is now a good time to talk, or would it be better if I called back later?" If they opt for a later time, find out the best time for you to return their call.

Things NOT to Say To Someone Who Has Cancer

When someone learns they have cancer, they can feel like they've lost control of their life. They see their plans, hopes, and dreams for the future slipping through their fingers. Being told what to do or how to act only magnifies this feeling. Some of the things on this list may surprise you, but they are things that patients and their caregivers commonly list as causing frustration and hurt.

"I know just how you feel."
Do you, really? Everyone is different. Even if you have been in a similar situation, saying that you know just how they feel demeans what the patient is going through. Instead, let them know that you have no idea of how they feel, but you can imagine it is extremely difficult. And that you would like to be there to support them during this time.

"That's what happens when you smoke two packs a day."

Never bring up behaviors (past or present) that might have contributed to his or her disease, such as smoking or drinking. They are fully aware of these things and often feel guilty about them already. To say something like this implies that you are callous to their plight and that they, essentially, deserve to have a deadly disease.

It is this type of logic that has caused lung cancer, the cancer that kills the most people each year, to receive the least amount of money to research treatments. No one deserves cancer.

"How long do you have?"

It's normal to be curious about what the future has in store for your friend. This can become an emotionally charged issue, especially if the doctor has told them the future looks grim. Some people even choose not to learn their own prognosis. Prognoses are wrong all the time. Asking this assumes the hopelessness of the situation, rather than allowing the patient to experience his own level of hope or lack of hope. The chances are, your friend will share what they know when they're ready. Instead ask, "Is there anything I can do to help you?"

"I'm sure you'll be fine."
"Think positive."
"Don't worry."
"This too shall pass."
"Things will get better"

There is nothing good about cancer. A person can (and should) choose to look at the blessings they have in their life, rather than dwell on cancer, but that doesn't happen with a pat on the back and a casual remark. The deep loss associated with cancer triggers the grief process in survivors and caregivers. This involves sadness and at times, anger. If you catch someone on a bad day, they'll want nothing to do with positivity.

A cancer diagnosis can induce a lot of worry and concern—and with good reason. Often, our first instinct when we hear that a friend has cancer is to reassure them. We have a natural desire to calm these fears. While phrases like these may seem uplifting and are often said to encourage the patient or caregiver, they can feel dismissive as they belittle their fears and feelings.

These common phrases give patients and caregivers the impression that the person saying them has no idea of what the patient is facing. They don't take into account the serious, life-threatening nature of cancer. These things are especially frustrating to patients and caregivers when the prognosis is grim. They can make them feel very alone and indicate that the speaker has no understanding of what is at stake.

You can't sweep cancer under the rug, so it's best not to try. Fight the urge to speak soothing words and instead, just listen. Say something from the list of helpful things to say. A better alternative would be to say something like, "I am so sorry to hear that. How are you doing with this?

"I know just what you should do."

It's common for friends and even strangers to suggest how a patient should deal with their cancer. In fact, it's one of the most frustrating things for patients and caregivers. While these ideas and "cures" come from a place of concern, they undervalue the situation by slapping an easy-fix on it.

Before giving advice, consider if it's even appropriate. How important is it that you share this pearl of wisdom? Even though advice is usually meant to be helpful, it can easily cause a rift in your relationship. Along with proposing what your friend would be better off doing, you are also implying that you know more than the patient and their medical team. It implies they aren't as smart as you and that you could run their life better than they are. Giving someone unsolicited advice is usually unwelcome and irritating.

Just because your friend is expressing their fears, or is sharing the decisions they face, it doesn't mean they want to hear your opinion on the matter. They are more likely looking for a listening ear.

If they do want your advice, they will ask for it directly. Even then, proceed with caution. Let them know that you would have to think long and hard about it before answering. This shows that you appreciate the gravity of what they face. If you just shoot from the hip and give them your thoughts without a long period of contemplation, you send the message that it's simple. They've been agonizing over this thing and you have the answer in ten seconds.

Even if you've given the matter a lot of thought, you don't necessarily need to share your opinion. This is especially true when your friend is considering their treatment options. Their decision could mean the difference between life and death, two months or twelve, painful side effects or few side effects, going into debt or staying financially stable. Many things are at stake. How one chooses between these priorities is very personal. For example, one person may want to survive until their child graduates in 18 months, even if it means enduring difficult treatments. Another may decide that they want to enter hospice immediately.

The patient and caregiver(s) are thinking about this new diagnosis every waking hour. They are researching and weighing their options as a family and with their trusted medical team. They don't make these decisions lightly. But they do often question their own decisions. Giving them your advice (which is often not applicable to their specific situation) can make this process more difficult.

Sometimes there are even disagreements within a family as to how (or whether) a particular treatment should be approached. Outside suggestions can stir up tension and pain. A wedge may form between you and your friend if they decide not to take your advice. This can happen if they feel like they've let you down, or that you are pushing an agenda, rather than being a friend.

Even worse, some claimed "cures" have resulted in patients who have otherwise treatable cancers, relying on false promises rather than treatments that can save their life. Do you really want that on your shoulders? If you do, ask permission and make sure your advice is welcome. Ultimately, medical decisions rest with the patient.

Doubting a patient's wisdom is demeaning. Giving a cancer patient advice in any form, without being asked to give it, could easily rub them the wrong way. It often comes off as pushy and condescending. Instead of giving advice, ask for advice about something about which your friend is knowledgeable. This helps him/her maintain an active role in your friendship. Just because your friend has cancer, doesn't mean their need to help and be heard has gone away.

"If you have faith God will heal you."

Saying things like this can spark another type of guilt; one that's related to the patient's faith. The deeper the person's faith, the more painful this well-meaning phrase can be. If his or her health begins to decline or a treatment isn't working, they may begin to wonder if it's due to their lack of faith. This can cause a lot of inner struggle for a Christian.

On one occasion my husband shared a story on social media about a man who died of cancer. Just hours before he died, his daughter was married at his bedside. Someone we know responded, "That Is a Sad Story, but Not you, you have overcome! Sorry to see other people don't have the knowledge, the blood of the Lamb, and the word of God to fight. Keep on fighting, you've got this!" [sic] The implication seemed to be that this man must not be a Christian, or that if he had more faith, he wouldn't be dying.

If someone doesn't have faith in God, these types of sentiments will mean little to them anyway, so it's best to leave this one alone altogether.

"Stay strong!"
"You've got to just keep fighting."
"You can do this."
"Never give up!"

It's natural to want to encourage someone in the battle for their life. It's what we do whenever a friend is facing any struggle. However, it can place an undue burden on the patient and their family.

Remember the comment someone made on my husband's social media? "....Keep on fighting, you've got this!" Statements like this imply that there is a failure in dying and that one must "fight."

These sentiments can make the patient feel guilty for wanting to discontinue their treatment. They may also feel like you didn't really listen to them as they expressed their feelings. Instead of being a cheerleader, listen to your friend. Support your friend's feelings. Allow them to be negative, withdrawn, or silent if they need to be. Resist the urge to change the subject. Silence and holding their hand can be a greater comfort than the most eloquent words.

Telling patients they are strong can cause them to act strong even when they are exhausted. While this might seem like a good idea, there are times when a patient needs to rest from active treatment. If and when they are ready to resume, they will be stronger for it. They will also appreciate knowing that whether they treat, or don't treat their cancer, you are there for them.

Our Story

After two years of cancer, Dan was worn out. He'd been on several treatments, one after another, and non-stop. His body was ravaged by cancer and chemotherapy.

From the beginning, I'd pushed him to never let up. But it was time for a break. He knew that he needed a couple of weeks off of the treatment, but he was afraid of disappointing me. He was so relieved when I told him that if he needed to rest from treatment, he should. It was then that I realized how much pressure he felt to fight as hard as possible in order to not worried he was about letting me down.

Most people have no idea how much pressure cancer patients feel as they make treatment decisions. This is an area where we need to tread lightly when supporting a friend who has cancer, or any other life-altering diagnosis.

Even if someone was motivated to "fight" at the beginning of their cancer journey, that could change if treatment is no longer effective and the cancer begins to progress. If their cancer is incurable, there will come a time when they start to lose the war. They may feel like they've disappointed people who thought that they could beat cancer.

The Battle

When you have treatable cancer, the metaphor of the battle can be empowering. It may be why we see cancer in terms of an enemy we must fight, conquer, and eradicate. There is a lot of truth in that rallying cry.

Unfortunately, the battle metaphor implies winners and losers. When someone has a terminal illness, they will ultimately "lose the battle." What if they've decided to stop fighting? It's helpful to think in bigger terms. Everyone will die at some point. When the patient is ready to die and is at peace with this it is a victory. Regardless of where the patient is in their cancer journey, it's best to avoid these emotionally charged words.

All of these suggestions are meant as guidelines, rather than hard and fast rules to be followed. If you speak from the heart and listen more than you talk, you will be fine. The most important thing is to keep in touch with your friend. It will mean a lot to them.

Helpful Things You CAN Say

It's difficult to know what to say when a friend or family member tells you they have cancer. After all, there's nothing you can say or do that will change their diagnosis. You might even feel like you need to make sense of it. If it could happen to them, it could happen to you. So, you search for some logical reason.

All too often, people talk when they should be listening. Your friend's life has just been turned upside down. One of the things they need most is to be able to share how they're feeling with someone. It can be difficult to hear the raw feelings your friend may express. Still, your attentive ear can be the best thing you can give him/her.

Learn about your friend's diagnosis. It can help to learn about your friend's diagnosis. Ask them if they want to talk about it. Most patients welcome the opportunity to share what they are experiencing, but some may not want to talk about the details. Keep in mind that five different people have five different versions of the same disease. No two experiences are alike, due to many factors.

Even when the diagnosis is the same, no two people respond exactly alike to treatment. All cancers are serious. Don't make the mistake of comparing one person's illness to someone else's.

Check-in periodically, with a phone call to let your friend know that you are thinking about them. It can be easy to forget to call, so ask what time of day it's best to call and schedule it in your calendar. When you do get a chance to talk, before asking personal questions, find out if they're welcome. Your friend or their caregiver will likely be happy to answer, but they may wish to keep some things private.

Now, what exactly should you say? Here are some ideas:

"I don't know what to say."
"I'm sorry you are going through this."

What you say isn't nearly as important as the fact that you care enough to be there and listen. The simplicity of either one of these phrases is the perfect way to let someone know you realize there are no easy answers. It tells them they can count on you during this hard time. And it's certainly better than not calling or visiting out of fear or discomfort. This means more than you may think. There are no expectations or pressures put on the patient. Instead, you acknowledge that the situation is terrible and that you care. This approach can be very meaningful.

"What are you thinking of doing?"
"If you ever feel like talking, I'll be here to listen."

Don't question their wisdom when they tell you their plan (or lack of one). Supporting their plan, even if you don't understand it, shows respect for the patient and their decision-making process. Adding your own opinions would only cause the patient to second guess themselves and the decisions they've put so much thought and research into making. Besides, do you really want to be responsible for someone else's life and death decisions? Don't give advice unless asked, and then, be reserved and careful.

"Is there any way that I can help?"
"Please think of something I can do for you. I will call you later this week to make a plan."
If there's something specific you would like to do, offer. Even if they decline, they will know that you care about them. If you want to do something but aren't sure what you can do to help, keep reading. You'll find plenty of ideas as you read this book. Your friend or their caregiver may have an idea or two of their own that you can help out with. We will dive deeper into this in the chapter, *Doing Something Helpful*.

"I'm thinking about you."
"You're in my thoughts and prayers."
These are also appropriate in a card or email. Often people assume that the patient has a lot of friends helping them through their illness, so they don't want to bother them. Unfortunately, many times others make the same assumption and the patient has no solid support system. Your encouragement will mean so much to the patient, their caregiver, and their family.

Tell the caregiver they are on your mind, as well. Often, the patient gets most of the support. Reminding the caregiver and other family members that you know they are going through their own whirlwind can help them to feel less alone. Saying this assures them that if they need a friend to talk to, they can count on you.

"I am going to be praying for you."

"I'm praying/hoping/wishing for you to find comfort and peace in your situation."

"I wish you the best possible outcome."

This idea is meant for praying people. It also supposes that your friend would appreciate your prayers. If you are unsure, there is no harm in asking, "Is it okay if I keep you in my prayers?" This sensitivity will likely be appreciated. If you tell them you will be praying for them, remember to actually pray. If you are in the same faith community and are both comfortable with it, you can say a short prayer for them at the end of your visit.

Never be a spiritual bully. I've known people who were driven away from their faith by a well-intentioned friend who was pushy and disrespectful as they warned an ill patient of fire and brimstone. I've also seen people take the faith they'd let simmer on the back burner and embrace it with fervor because of a friend who showed them respect and love in their time of need.

"We are having a dinner for some close friends in a month. We'd love it if you could come."

Don't be afraid to make future plans. When making plans, be flexible in case an appointment or feeling unwell interferes and your friend needs to cancel or reschedule. The great thing about future plans is that they give your friend something to look forward to.

Doing Something Helpful

Hearing that someone you care about has cancer can leave you feeling powerless. How can you help when what they face is so devastating?

I recall what it was like before Dan was diagnosed, to hear about life-altering things that people experienced, such as the death of a spouse, a terminal diagnosis, or a tragic accident. I always assumed that there was a throng of support standing on their doorstep. I thought that a call from me would only interrupt their routine and that surely my well-wishes wouldn't make a dent in what they were feeling. It was even more intimidating when it was someone I didn't know well.

I still struggle with feelings of inadequacy when it comes to helping people in these situations, even after experiencing the impact that these things can have. I remind myself how much I appreciate gestures of support from strangers, acquaintances, and friends, alike.

Like me, you may feel overwhelmed in the face of such crushing pain. Where do you start? As you read this chapter, highlight or write down the ideas that seem doable for you. Not every idea will be for you, but you'll find many things that you can feel comfortable and confident about doing. You may even decide to stretch yourself by trying other ways of being a supportive friend.

Unfortunately, many patients and caregivers find their circle of friends suddenly shrinks when they are diagnosed. This often happens because people think that other family, friends, and professionals are helping out.

You might feel like you would only be in the way, but many people don't have much of a support system, to begin with. Family members, who would normally be there for them, may live far away. Often patients don't want to be a bother so they don't tell anyone about their needs. Some have friends and family who don't know how to be helpful (or choose not to be). Whatever their situation, they are sure to appreciate your desire to be there for them at this difficult time. It's safe to assume your help is needed.

"I wish there was something I could do to help"

Some patients and caregivers find it hard to accept support – even when they need it. Don't be surprised or hurt if your friend declines your offer to help. It's not you. It's often more about their pride and their need for independence. Remind them that you want to do it because you care. You'd take away the cancer if you could, but you can't, so this is your way of trying to ease their burden. When put into those terms, it makes sense to accept help.

Make your offer specific. When a person first gets a cancer diagnosis, they're often so overwhelmed that they have no idea how to ask for help or what to ask for. They can experience this at other times in their cancer journey, as well. There are times when patients and caregivers feel so paralyzed by what they are going through, that it's difficult for them to decide what would be most helpful.

Often if the offer is vague and requires the patient or caregiver to think of what they need help with, they will feel like a deer caught in the headlights, unable to decide which direction to go. Instead of making a vague, "Call me when you need me," offer, make your friend's life easier by offering to help with specific tasks, such as taking care of children, pets, or preparing a meal. If they decline help, be sure to offer another form of help later.

If the patient says that they don't need any help, check in with the caregiver (even if you don't know the caregiver well). While the patient may be turning away offers of help, the caregiver might not be receiving any. Patients can become so caught up in their illness (understandably) that they may not realize many of the things they once did around the home, are now being handled by their caregiver. This often contributes to caregiver burnout.

If you commit to helping, it's important to follow through. If something urgent comes up that interferes with your plans, let them know immediately. If possible, reschedule or make other arrangements for things like meals. They are counting on you to keep your promises. Let them know you're on-call for any emergency that may arise and repeat the offer in the future. Even if they say no, over and over again, at some point, they may take you up on your offer. And, even if they don't, they will know that you care.

Projects around the House

When my husband was diagnosed with stage IV lung cancer, we were left with endless questions about the future. We were renters at the time. Dan wanted to ensure that we would have an affordable home to live in, one where we had shared memories. Soon, we became homeowners.

We purchased a townhome so we wouldn't need to worry about yard work or shoveling. Still, lots of remodeling needed to be done to prepare our new two-bedroom home for our family. Friends of ours, carpenters, an electrician, and folks skilled at sheet-rocking, painting, and laying down vinyl flooring, worked for a month to make the house our home. We were so humbled by the love these people poured into the work they did.

It wasn't the only time we were helped by family and friends. During Dan's difficult chemotherapy treatments, people drove our daughter to and from school and brought us meals.

Double-Coupon Tuesday

Since marrying my husband, I'd only filled our car's gas tank once. It may seem silly to some people. After all, I'm perfectly capable of filling a car's gas tank, but Dan has always said that as long as he was around, I would never have to smell like gasoline.

It was a Tuesday (double-coupon day at the gas station), the day that Dan always filled the cars' gas tanks. Our tanks were empty from a week of driving to appointments and running our daughter to college. Dan was particularly ill. Still, he pulled on his jeans and grabbed the car keys to head to the gas station.

When I tried to talk him out of going, saying I would fill the cars, he insisted that he may not be able to do much for me, as sick as he, but he could keep his word that I wouldn't have to pump gas. I could see how important it was to him. He deserved to keep his honor and dignity intact. Weak and nauseous, he drove both vehicles to the station and filled our tanks.

While he was gone, his sister and our brother-in-law arrived to drop off a meal and pray with us. I told them why Dan was gone and how he was feeling. My brother in law said, "If you ever need anything, including filling your car's gas tanks, just call me." He meant it. While I've never had to call him to fill our gas tanks, just knowing that he'd be there if I did, means everything.

A Birthday Save

When our youngest daughter turned 12 my husband was so ill that we didn't expect him to live for much longer. I was exhausted and we were stretched to our limits. I posted a request on our *CaringBridge* blog. "Could someone help us by making a meal or a cake?"

A friend of ours, whose husband was also a cancer survivor, came to the rescue. She made hamburgers and even a cake themed after my daughter's favorite TV show, *Doctor Who*. Our daughter had an amazing birthday and I didn't feel mom-guilt.

There are many things you can do for a friend facing a health crisis. Plan projects in advance and start them only after talking with the caregiver. This will help things go as smoothly as possible for everyone.

Ask the patient or caregiver for a list of things they need help with and which tasks would make the biggest difference. Then, organize family, friends, neighbors, and co-workers who are willing to help complete the tasks on a regular, weekly basis.

Delegate jobs from this list and prioritize any urgent errands or projects. There are websites that can help with this. My favorite is *caringbridge.org*. It is well known as a no-cost, easy way for patients to share their health journey with family and friends. It also has a built-in planner designed to organize meals, rides, childcare, and other types of assistance. Often patients and caregivers ask a friend to help maintain the site by sharing updates and manage requests.

Countless Ways to Help

- Fill their car's gas tank. This helps them financially and takes care of a task which can be hard to do when they feel nauseous.

- Provide a meal for a patient and their family. If your friend is getting chemo, ask what they feel like eating since the chemo often affects taste buds and appetite.

- Schedule a night of takeout food and a DVD for the patient and their family.

- Organize a support team to check on your friend regularly and help with things around the house.

- Drive your friend to an appointment. Offer to take notes during an appointment or provide company during their treatment.

- Go for a walk together.

- Think about the little things your friend enjoys doing that make life feel "normal" for them. Find ways to make these activities easier.

- Offer to make any difficult phone calls. Or, gather information about different resources they may need.

- Set up a fundraiser. This could be a picnic where people come to donate money or a *Go Fund Me* campaign. There are also home-party fundraisers offered by direct sales companies that donate a percentage of the sales to the cause of your choice.

- Care for your friend's lawn or garden once a month.

- Baby-sit, pet-sit, or take care of your friend's plants.

- Return or pick up books, movies, or books on CD from the library. Patients can check them out online.

- Buy groceries.

- Go to the post office.

- Pick up prescriptions.

- Drive family or friends to and from the airport or a hotel.

- Clean your friend's home for an hour every Saturday. Or, hire a housekeeper to clean their home. If it's financially prohibitive, ask other friends to chip in to cover the cost. Take care of the details so they just need to be there to open the door.

- Do laundry once a week.

- Take the patient or caregiver out. They might enjoy a baseball game, a movie, or a fancy cup of coffee and conversation. Whatever you do will be appreciated, because you're together.

As you spend time with your friend and learn more about how cancer is affecting their everyday life, keep your eyes open for other things you can offer to do. See how your friend responds to different activities and know that the situation may change as treatment goes on. Tailoring your help to what they need and enjoy most, is the best way to be a good friend.

Special Skills You May Have

Often, people feel like they have nothing to offer. We all have some talent that we can put to use when the time is right. Over the years our lives have been touched by things that people have done for our family, using their unique gifts and special skills. Here are just a few examples.

Pictures

Our daughters met a professional photographer at an event for families facing cancer. The photographer later spoke with the event coordinator and asked if they could reach out to us. She wanted to offer her services by giving our family a free photo session in her studio. She took hundreds of poses. One of the photos is even on the cover of my book, *Facing Cancer as a Parent: Helping Your Child Cope with Your Cancer.*

You don't have to be a professional photographer to help capture memories. My husband's sister is very skilled with a camera. So when our daughter, Summer, was in her senior year of high school, my sister-in-law brought her to a local park and took her senior pictures.

Step-by-Step

With the help of wonderful friends and family, we replaced the carpet in our home with engineered hardwood floors. We had to remove the wrought iron railings that separated the living room from the entryway in our split-level townhome. We decided to replace them with oak railings.

Dan stained and varnished all of the railings and spindles. But the installation had to be done professionally and would cost way more than we realized. Because we didn't have the money to hire a professional, the railings and the spindles sat in the garage for months. Then, the cancer in Dan's body went wild. There would be no stopping it. He had multiple trips to the hospital in just a couple of months. Eventually, he would leave the hospital for the last time to begin in-home hospice.

The day before he came home, one of his life-long friends (a professional contractor) and his wife spent an entire day installing the railings. They were beautiful. And best of all, they would keep our family, friends, and the hospice team, safe from falls.

The Sound of Music

While my husband was on hospice, two different musicians gave us the gift of music. The first was a fellow Realtor we work with at our Real Estate company. He and his wife are a Real Estate team like Dan and I. So over the years we've become close.

They came over together to pray with us, to bring a meal for our family, and share some music. He played in a blues-rock style that really lifted our spirits.

Another friend and her family came over with the intention of singing and playing guitar for Dan. This couple brought a big pot of soup for our family to have for dinner. She pulled out the most beautiful and unique guitar and began to sing. Her voice was like an angel's. When Dan died, she sang at his funeral. She also wrote a beautiful song in his honor for me.

The Gift of Memories

We were told that when someone dies who is in your immediate family, you will barely remember the funeral because of the effect grief has on your brain. Because of that, it's a good idea to videotape the funeral. Later, when you are ready to watch it, it is incredibly meaningful.

We talked about this before Dan died. He mentioned a young man whose parents had been long-time friends of ours. Perhaps he would video the funeral.

Somehow this slipped my mind when Dan died and we began making arrangements. I started looking everywhere for someone to record the funeral, even putting the word out on social media. Then, one night I got a text message from that young man. He'd heard I was looking for a videographer, and it turned out that he was trained! It was such a relief to know that we would have this special memory of Dan's funeral and that it would be well put together. It was even more special because he was the person Dan would have chosen.

If you have a special skill that you can use to help a family facing cancer, you should use it. But don't make the mistake of thinking that you have nothing to offer. Just giving the gift of your time and love is a wonderful thing that won't be forgotten.

Bringing Meals

"Life expectancy would grow by leaps and bounds if green vegetables smelled as good as bacon."
~Doug Larson

I was Hungry and You Fed Me
Whether you're facing cancer as a patient or a spouse, thinking about what you're going to make for dinner is the last thing on your mind. Our daughters were 8, 10, and 14 when Dan was diagnosed. I was homeschooling them, juggling appointments, and dealing with responsibilities at the church my husband pastored. Inevitably, the dinner hour would arrive and I'd realize that I hadn't planned a meal for the family (Unfortunately, this still happens). My children were scrounging in the cupboards because I had dropped the ball. I felt like a failure as a wife and as a mother.

Thankfully, family members and friends took turns bringing meals over to get us through that time. This made a huge difference. Some meals were simple, such as a casserole. Some were extravagant and even included dessert. Some people brought homemade meals, and others brought meals from restaurants or stores. They all served the same purpose. They nourished us and alleviated the guilt I felt for not being on top of things enough to think ahead. These meals also helped our budget which was stretched thin due to my husband's cancer. Every one of them was appreciated.

The following are some suggestions to help make your gift of a meal a hit. You don't have to use all of them. Incorporating even a few will help your friend, greatly.

Some Suggestions
- Ask what's for dinner. Does anyone in the family have a dietary restriction? Sometimes treatments affect a patient's diet or someone in the family has a food allergy. Are there favorite foods? Finding out the answers to these questions can make the meal a complete success. You may even want to ask what they're in the mood for and treat them to something they've been craving.

- "When should I stop by?" Check on which day and time would be best for a meal. This ensures that the patient is getting a meal when they need it most. If you need to drop it off at a time when there's no one available to accept the meal, such as during an appointment, a Styrofoam cooler is perfect for keeping cold food cold and hot food hot (just not at the same time). Our family asked for meals on the days Dan had chemo, and the following 2 days as well since they were a roller coaster of sickness and sleepless nights. Those dinners kept us going.

- Put food in disposable containers when possible. There are several brands of disposable containers that can be used. Ice cream buckets are perfect for soup. While these containers can be reused, you can let your friend know that there's no need to return them. This will take that concern off their shoulders. It is one more thing that your friend won't need to keep track of. If you do bring any dishes over that you'd like returned, let your friend know that you'll pick them up on a particular date. If they won't be home that day, they can just leave them in a bag on the doorstep.

- If you're using a crock-pot, there are a couple of things that you can do to make this an easier experience. Use the slow cooker bags (sold in the same aisle as the foil and plastic wrap). They make cleaning a crockpot so much easier. Also, like in the last suggestion, offer to pick up the crock-pot in a few days. I know one lady that stocks up on crockpots she gets on Black Friday and at garage sales for about $5. This enables her to tell her friends that they can keep the crockpot.

- If you are making a meal that is baked in a pan, purchase disposable foil pans to make cleanup easier, and to eliminate the need for your friend to have to return the pan.

- Consider doing the dishes. Disposable dishes allow the patient and their family to clean up with no soap and water necessary. This means that the patient and their family have one less thing to deal with after the meal is over. To reduce the impact that disposable dishes have on the environment, you can purchase eco-friendly dishes and cutlery.

- When you deliver a meal, stay for a (short, 5 minute) visit, or just drop off the food if they're not up for chatting.

- Deliver an extra pre-made meal that your friend can heat up as needed. It could be a frozen meal or a heat and eat option. Soups and casseroles are great freezable meals. This means your friend will have dinner available in the future. Use storage containers that don't need to be returned.

- Sometimes things don't go as planned. You've offered to bring a meal, and then, you are asked to work late that day, or your car breaks down—or both. You know the kind of day I'm talking about. Simplify things by having a pizza or another type of take-out sent to your friend. Rotisserie chicken from the deli is a delicious, healthy option, as well.

- Organize a meal schedule for your friend. Some online communities like *takethemameal.com*, *lotsahelpinghands.com*, or *caringbridge.org* can help manage meal schedules. The old-fashioned method of writing activities and commitments by hand into a paper calendar works well, too. Make sure your friend has access to the calendar so he or she knows what to expect, and when.

- Gift Cards to restaurants are a fantastic way to provide a meal, and a night out. When we were courting, my husband vowed to take me on a date once a week for the rest of our lives. Some weeks, going on our date for an hour was the only time, other than appointments, that we got out of the house together. These dates helped us to feel more human. Often we were able to do it thanks to one of the generous friends who gave us a gift card. Gift cards can also be used for meal delivery and pick up. Most chain restaurants now have a to-go option. Your friend can order their favorite meal online with a gift card, and have someone pick it up for them. This is a good option if you have a long-distance friend who is facing cancer.

One last thing...
Sometimes, the recipient of your meal doesn't get a chance to thank you. This is often because they can't remember what day it is, let alone if they have sent a thank you card. Sometimes, they are so busy that traditional manners take a back seat.

I never knew how amazing a delivered meal was, until the first time we had one. Each meal we received was the difference between feeling guilty when the kids asked what was for dinner and being able to sit down as a family together with no added stress. It may have even been the difference between eating and not eating. As I type this now, I am tearing up with gratitude as I think back on the meals that have come through our door.

Gifts

I'm a terrible gift-giver. Each Christmas my sisters-in-law and I all exchange gifts. They are little gift bags of things that make life fun: notebooks, lotions, great pens, etc. I am always in awe of the ladies' creativity and thoughtfulness. In comparison, my ideas are unoriginal, and my gift bags aren't nearly as cute. Still, they appreciate my effort.

Gifts are another way to show someone you care about them. They can be practical, fun, interesting, serious, or light, depending on what your friend needs the most. And they don't have to be perfect. When giving gifts, it's helpful to keep in mind your friend's interests and hobbies. They may appreciate something silly or unusual, or something deeply meaningful. If the patient is someone you don't know as well, like a neighbor or work colleague, you may want to stick with something more traditional.

Gifts We've Received

We've received some gifts that have lightened our load during this journey. Gift cards to order pizza enabled us to make our daughter's 11th birthday more special, even though we were financially strapped.

One day a dear couple stopped by with a pair of slippers, a robe, comfy pajama bottoms, and several meals for the freezer. Another time, this same couple took our family to the movie theater. We were overwhelmed by their love for us.

Another couple came over during the holidays with a basket full of fruit, and a gift card for groceries which we used in order to have a wonderful Christmas meal with all our kids.

For some people, this love language comes easily. If you are more like me than these gifted gift-givers, read on for some great gift-giving ideas that you can use to support your friend who is facing cancer.

Money

Money can be a sensitive subject, but it is an important part of life. Even when a patient has a job that provides sick pay, it quickly runs out leaving them with no income. Self-employed people don't have sick-pay or paid time off.

The patient's spouse needs to be there for the patient during treatment and recovery. When someone is facing an illness that can be terminal, it's important for them to have as much time with their family as possible, especially when there are children at home. Having both parents available to manage their children's insecurities and other by-products of the situation can make a big difference.

You can learn more about parenting with cancer in my book, *Facing Cancer as a Parent: Helping Your Children Cope with Your Cancer.*

Gift Cards

Gift certificates for massage, spa services, restaurants, or museum/art gallery passes can all help lift someone's spirits and make life a little more normal.

Gift cards to grocery stores can help with the expense of food.

Buy gas cards to help with the extra driving to appointments. I remember one week when we spent about 10 hours driving to and from appointments. Gas cards given to us made a huge difference!

Digital Gifts

Digital music or audiobooks are a great way to pass the time in the chemo chair. One of the side effects of chemo is that it can make it difficult to concentrate on reading. Just being able to listen to music or a good book can be relaxing and uplifting.

Video streaming service or DVDs of movies, TV shows, or documentaries are also a great way to pass the time together for patients and caregivers.

A video message from family and friends can really brighten the day of a hospital or home-bound patient. Thanks to smartphones, they are easier than ever to record and send. Pictures of friends and family are another great option.

A tablet and a gift card to add some games, music, movies or books to it is an incredibly thoughtful gift that would be appreciated by anyone.

Traditional Comfort Gifts
A good book or a magazine or newspaper subscription is perfect for friends who love to read.

Crossword or Sudoku puzzles help patients and caregivers pass the time in waiting rooms and chemo chairs.

Notecards or a journal can help your friend respond to snail mail and record their thoughts during this life-changing journey.

A plant or flowers can brighten up a hospital room or a home. However, make sure the person isn't on neutropenia precautions first (just ask the patient or caregiver if flowers are okay). Fresh flowers can be an infection risk for cancer patients with weakened immune systems. At the same time, make sure they don't have any sensitivity. Lilies, in particular, can have beautiful, but strong scents that bother some people who are prone to migraines.

Splurge and Pamper
Accessories (necklaces, bracelets, scarves, ties, hats), makeup, or beauty item can help patients look their best at a time when treatments can make this more difficult.

Portable hobby supply kits (scrapbooking, drawing, and needlepoint) or puzzles can be relaxing gifts.

A soft, comfortable hat or scarf if your friend will lose his/her hair with treatment helps men and women feel more comfortable in appearance, and physically. You lose a lot of heat through your head when you don't have hair, and in the summer, there is an increased risk of sunburn.

Slippers, pajamas, a super comfy blanket, socks, or robe, are perfect for couch lounging or trips to chemo.

Paid Services

Treat him or her to a spa or beauty treatment: manicure/pedicure, facial, makeup application, etc. It may be the first time they've felt pampered in a while.

Housecleaning- When someone has cancer, the entire household goes into survival mode, and cleaning often falls by the wayside. But that doesn't mean that the newly accumulated dust and clutter go unnoticed. Often, patients and caregivers are embarrassed at the condition of their home because they lack the time and energy to clean. They scurry around trying to get things in order when they know that someone is stopping by, only to be exhausted later.

If your friend mentions that they are having a hard time keeping up with housework, you could offer to help, either hands-on or by paying for a visit from a cleaning service on chemo day. They could return home to a spiffed-up house and have one less thing to worry about. Use your best judgment as to how this will be received. Some people are very private, and often shame and embarrassment will keep people from accepting.

Send a mobile masseuse for a gift massage. Use caution if the patient has metastatic cancer that has spread to their lymphatic system. The safest thing to do is to have them check with their doctor to ensure that a massage is safe for them. This is also a great gift for stressed-out caregivers.

If you want to give outside of the box

Look into donating air miles so that they can take a trip, or family from far away can visit.

Check to see if your employer would allow you to donate vacation time to cover paid-time-off hours for the patient or caregiver you work with. If they are okay with this, other co-workers may want to contribute hours, as well.

Gifts: A Chemo Day Bag

Spending time in the chemo chair is no fun. Chemo day often includes several different appointments that can really draw out an already long day. Why not give your friend a bag filled with things that can make the time go by faster?

Any bag will do. A canvas tote bag, a backpack, or a small gym bag will do the trick. If you are going to go all out, a diaper bag (a neutral one, without a baby motif) has plenty of room, and all the pockets are great for organizing the goodies you can fill it with. Even a small gift bag with one or two items will let the patient know you care and want to make their chemo day easier.

Things you can include
- A travel mug with herbal tea or cocoa packets

- Lotion and lip balm help with the drying effect of chemo.

- Mints, lemon drops or ginger candy, all help with nausea associated with chemotherapy.

- A favorite novel, puzzle book or devotional can help pass the hours in the chair. Add a journal and pen for the patient to record their thoughts at such an emotional time.

- Hand sanitizer and baby wipes are wonderful for cleaning up after a snack (which you could also include).

- If you really feel like going all out, you could add a quilt or a fleece blanket.

- A heating pad is a great addition for extra comfort and warmth during those long chemo sessions.

- Consider putting together a small bag for the caregiver. Often, they sit in a folding chair during the hours the patient is receiving chemo.

Our Story

Two years after Dan was initially diagnosed with cancer, he developed brain metastases. We needed to go to the University of Minnesota so that he could have a procedure called, Gamma Knife. The procedure used concentrated rays of radiation to strategically eliminate the tumor while sparing the rest of the brain.

It was going to be a long day. My sister-in-law sent two little gift bags, one for me and one for my mother-in-law who accompanied us. They contained snacks and reading material for us while we waited. This made a frightening day easier.

Caregivers and Children

An estimated 44 million Americans ages 18 and older provide unpaid assistance and support to adults with disabilities and elderly who live in the community. The value of this unpaid labor force is estimated to be at least $306 billion annually, nearly double the combined costs of home health care ($43 billion) and nursing home care ($115 billion). In most cases, the primary caregiver is a spouse, partner, or an adult child. If a patient doesn't have family nearby, close friends, co-workers, or neighbors sometimes fill this role. Good, reliable caregiver support is crucial to the physical and emotional well-being of people with cancer.

Who Cares for the Caregiver?
Often, caregivers spend so much time taking care of the patient and the patient's responsibilities that they forget to take care of themselves. It's often difficult for them to fit exercise into their schedule and eating well takes a back seat. It's common for a caregiver to feel guilty if they take

the time to pursue a hobby or just take time for themselves on a regular basis.

Many caregivers have a positive experience. They feel a sense of accomplishment and even joy at being able to help someone they love. Even with the benefits that can come from being a caregiver, they frequently experience burnout and caregiver stress. When you help a caregiver, you help a patient.

Signs and Symptoms of Burnout
- Feeling overwhelmed
- Feeling alone, isolated, or deserted by others
- Sleeping too much or too little
- Gaining or losing a lot of weight
- Feeling tired most of the time
- Losing interest in activities you used to enjoy
- Becoming easily irritated or angered
- Feeling worried or sad often
- Frequent headaches or body aches

Ways Stress Affects Caregivers

Depression and anxiety- Women who are caregivers are more likely than men to develop symptoms of anxiety and depression. Anxiety and depression also raise your risk for other health problems, such as heart disease and stroke.

Weakened immune system- Stressed caregivers may have weaker immune systems than non-caregivers and spend more days sick with the cold or flu. A weak immune system can also make vaccines such as flu shots less effective. Also, it may take longer to recover from surgery.

Obesity- Stress causes weight gain more often in women than in men. Obesity raises your risk for other health problems, including heart disease, stroke, and diabetes.

Higher risk for chronic diseases- High levels of stress, especially when combined with depression, can raise your risk for health problems, such as heart disease, cancer, diabetes, or arthritis.

Problems with short-term memory or paying attention- In particular, caregivers of spouses with Alzheimer's disease are at higher risk for problems with short-term memory and focus. This is also an issue for caregivers whose loved one has died. Griever's Brain affects both men and women and can be the result of any trauma or deep loss.

Some Suggestions
- Keep an eye out for signs of depression in the caregiver.

- Make sure the caregiver doesn't neglect their health. They should be making regular trips to the doctor and dentist.

- Caregivers can use a blog such as *caringbridge.org* or an email list can be used to update family and friends without having to repeat themselves so often. If they are overwhelmed by this, you could offer to start it and maintain it until they're ready to take it over. If you do this, prior to publishing, have the caregiver review any updates for accuracy and to ensure they are comfortable with posting the information.

- Allow the caregiver to vent. Many caregivers feel guilty expressing feelings of discouragement and frustration, so they keep them inside. By allowing them to express these feelings *without trying to fix the situation* is very helpful.

- Babysit their children. Take them to and from school and activities. Take the kids out for a couple of hours of fun. It can be an event or a trip to a restaurant, taking them out for ice cream, having them over for a sleepover, or just an hour in the park.

- Take children to dental and doctor's appointments. These appointments sometimes slip through the cracks of the busy schedule being maintained by exhausted parents. Ensuring the kids get their normal check-ups can prevent problems for them later on.

- Offer to bring children to their place of worship if the parents are unable to go.

- Spend time with the patient if they are too ill and unable to be left alone. This will give the caregiver a couple of hours to get out of the house or even to just take a much-needed nap. This time can be very renewing.

- Take the caregiver out for coffee or a lunch date.

- Schedule a weekly walk with the caregiver. This will help them get often needed exercise and fresh air. During inclement weather, you can walk in a mall. Often malls open early, before the stores do, so people can walk without the crowds.

- Offer to take them out to a movie. If they're too tired, drop off a DVD with some microwave popcorn and some beverages.

- Treat him or her to a spa day or a beauty treatment: manicure/pedicure, facial, makeup application, massage, etc. It may be the first time they've felt pampered in a while.

- Arrange for a hairstylist to make a home visit to trim the entire family's hair. This is something that's often put on a back burner in the chaos of caregiving.

- Call when you are en route to a store to see if you can pick anything up for their family.

- Say to the caregiver, "Give me a task. It could be laundry, cleaning your kitchen, or an errand like picking up groceries." Often, a patient will refuse the help that a caregiver greatly needs. Let them know that you can be in and out. No socializing needed (unless they would like some).

- Offer to clean one room of their house. Bring your own cleaning supplies so that you can get right down to work. He or she may want to participate. Many hands make light work and you can chat while you get the job done.

- Offer to wash/fold laundry.
- Wash and clean their car.

- Help with seasonal tasks like cleaning gutters, raking leaves, and shoveling.

- Donate money or vacation time to cover paid-time-off hours for the caregiver (some employers allow this).

- Donate air miles so they can take a trip or a family member from far away, with limited resources, can visit.

- Give them the book, *Facing Cancer as a Parent: Helping your Child Cope with Your Cancer.* This is another book in the *Facing Cancer* series. It looks at the unique aspects of living with cancer while also parenting young children.

- If you are a praying person, pray for the caregiver and any children the patient has. *If they would appreciate it*, tell the caregiver that they are in your prayers.

Use Care

One thing to note is that caregivers often feel sensitive to criticism. As you offer to help out, use care not to make it seem like you doubt the caregiver's ability to cope with the pressures of caregiving. Don't try to change the way the caregiver is running the household. Caregivers often worry that they aren't doing a good enough job. It's important that while you help, you don't reinforce these false thought processes.

Our Story

At the time Dan was diagnosed, I was a very private, introverted person. We hadn't been married long. I was a stay-at-home mom and didn't have many strong friendships. Dan was getting many emails and calls. I had gotten a total of two, so I felt very much alone.

That all changed with an email I received from my sister-in-law, Marion, on the evening of November 2, 2012.

Praying for you on THIS day, today—

That Dan's results would be given to you by the end of the day.

That the results would be so much better than expected.

That you would be able to get at least an idea of a treatment plan and what to expect in the coming weeks.

That you would physically feel the peace of the many, many people praying for you today as you wait.

That you would end the day encouraged, and filled with hope for your family's future.

Know that your family is deeply loved by God, by family and by friends.

Kevin, the girls and I had a family prayer meeting last night for all of you.

I felt so loved and cared for. Everything she had prayed in that email had been on my heart and mind. It seemed that God had moved her to write to me in my time of greatest need. It was then that I knew I wasn't alone. Since that time, Marion has become my best friend and biggest cheerleader. Her friendship has enabled me to be a good caregiver for Dan. She continued to send me encouraging emails, and while she and her family have done so much more for me and my family, I wanted to focus on this email. Such a simple thing can change someone's life.

I'll never forget the way I felt, knowing that someone cared at a time when I felt so alone. The irony is that she thought I had lots of support. She didn't realize what a difference her words would make.

I tell this story to encourage you to reach out to those people in your life who are caring for a cancer patient. They need to be lifted up, as well. The love you show them can make all the difference in the world.

Our Daughter, Sam

While researching for my book, *Facing Cancer as a Parent,* I interviewed my daughter, Sam, about what it's like to have a parent with cancer. I asked, what surprised her most about our experience.

She said, "How many people have supported us. I mean, I knew people would be there for us, but it has really been amazing, how wonderful they've been."

It's not just the patient who will be blessed by your support and care. It's their entire family who will benefit.

When Your Friend Has Died

When Dan died, I was so unprepared. You would think that after 6 ½ years of living with his cancer, we would have somehow prepared ourselves for the fact that he would one day die, but I don't think that anyone is really prepared to say goodbye to their spouse, their child, their mom or dad, sibling, or the friend they have known for so many years.

During the last month of Dan's life, he was on in-home hospice. Many people have a misconception of what hospice is. Hospice isn't a place. It's a set of services provided by a team of people. This team includes doctors, nurses, nursing assistants, a music therapy musician (if you choose), a chaplain (also, if you choose). You can also request a hospice volunteer, which we did. Our particular volunteer recorded conversations that Dan had with our children, one-on-one. These are precious keepsakes that we will always have.

As I said, hospice isn't a place. You can get these services in your home or, if you choose to pay for a facility (since they typically aren't covered by insurance) then you can receive the services in a skilled nursing facility.

For several reasons, Dan received hospice care in our home. Many people thought that we would have a nurse that could stay with him while I took a break, or overnight so I could sleep. This isn't the case. We had a nurse who came in about 3 times a week until the very end when she began to visit nearly every day. These visits lasted about an hour and consisted of dressing changes and vital signs as well as reassessing medications (which seemed to happen nearly every day).

Dan often forgot that he couldn't walk, so when he woke in the middle of the night he would take his oxygen off and try to get out of bed. I had to learn to sleep with one eye open since his oxygen was essential and it was unsafe for him to walk. I was completely exhausted.

The wonderful thing about having hospice in our home was the fact that it was convenient for family and friends to visit. After a couple of weeks, visits became very taxing for Dan so we had to limit them. Still, nearly every day there was a steady stream of people knocking on our door.

The day Dan died was the worst day the children and I have ever endured.

The next day I went to the funeral home and executed the decisions Dan had made as well as those he didn't (such as the verse that would go on his memorial card and the thank-you cards).

When I got home, everything we had used to care for him was gone: The hospital bed and table, the 5-150 lb. tanks of liquid oxygen, the wheelchair and the commode, everything. The medical supply company had come to retrieve it. This was good, but it also left the house feeling bare and empty.

The strangest thing was the lack of people. We had gotten so used to having a house full and now it was completely silent. It stayed that way for a long time.

In movies, I've seen neighbors and friends stop by a widow's home with casseroles and encouragement. Only 3 people came to my door. Thankfully they loved on me enough for a crowd.

I think that everyone in the family was grieving in their own way and that it hurt them to come to the last place they had seen Dan alive; the place where he had died. I also think that they were unsure of what the girls and I wanted. Did we need space? Did we have so much to deal with that we wouldn't have time to visit?

My sister-in-law came over to help make funeral arrangements. I don't know how I would have done it if it weren't for her and the other wonderful people working behind the scenes to get everything put together. My head was in such a fog.

The love we received from the church was so touching. The pastor who married Dan and I was retired, but he officiated at Dan's funeral. I was so thankful! Things came together in the end and Dan had a beautiful funeral.

I share this with you as a reminder that when someone dies, the family they leave behind is forever changed. It's more than dealing with financial decisions and broken appliances and tearful children. It's not being able to share with your best friend, the funny thing that happened on the way to the store. I will never be kissed goodnight again. Our youngest won't be taught how to drive by her dad. None of our kids will have him give them away on their wedding day or see him hold their baby. I question every decision because in the past we always made decisions together. I almost never drink coffee anymore because he always made our morning coffee and we would start our day together chatting at the kitchen table (the table we were going to refinish together, but I did it alone last month and pretty much ruined it).

Nothing is the same. Not one little thing about our lives has been unchanged.

But, I have surrounded myself with some wonderful friends, some new, some who have stuck by me through the years. They understand when I need my space and that I often need to be reminded that I'm not alone, because it can feel very lonely, even in a crowd.

When I bought my car only a couple of weeks after Dan died, some people thought I was doing something great, moving forward, so to speak. They didn't realize that my old car wouldn't start at the worst times. I had a client I needed to drive around and I certainly couldn't have us stuck somewhere with a car that wouldn't start. Buying a new car was the last thing I wanted to do. That was the kind of thing that Dan liked doing.

Everything seems so much harder without him because we used to have certain roles. He took care of the garage and the finances. I took care of the inside of the house. There was a very good reason for us to set up our life this way. We played to our strengths. Now, I have to learn all sorts of stuff that I was never good at, to begin with.

I've had many people say that it must be easier for me since I have the kids. I understand where they are coming from. The kids do keep me going in some ways. But they also each come with their own set of needs and issues surrounding the loss of their dad. And now I'm a single mom. Whoever said that would be easy?

What does this mean for you and the people who are left behind after a loved one dies of cancer? It means that it's important to not forget them. I've often heard that at funerals, but never realized how true it was until I experienced it, myself. By the time the flowers have died, people forget about you.

Interestingly, I have also learned from widows and grief counselors that the 2nd year is actually harder than the 1st. In the first year, people understand if you are having a hard time. The 2nd year they wonder why you haven't moved on, as if you ever can.

The things that I wrote about in the last chapter, *Caregivers and Children*, also apply to widows and children. This is especially true when a widow has children in the home. I will boil it down to 3 important things to do to help widows, children, and other close family members.

3 Things to Remember

1

Don't stay away. Sometimes widows and their children feel like lepers. No one knows what to say to them and what not to say. When in doubt, ask. "Would you like to talk about it?" is a great question. I wanted to talk about Dan all of the time. I still do. I want to keep his memory alive in conversation. Talking about him was healing for me. For our children, it hurt to talk about him in the beginning. So, asking is always a good thing.

2

Understand when they aren't playing their A-game. This is especially true in the first year after their loss. Their mind is fuzzy and they just don't think very clearly or remember things from one day to the next. This was one of the biggest surprises and frustrations for me after Dan died.

3

Remember the important days and ask if there is anything you can do to make them easier. Anniversaries, birthdays, holidays, even traditions like going to the cabin every year are never going to be the same. Is there something you can do? It may mean going out for lunch or maybe not mentioning the day at all. I have spoken to widows and widowers who have a vast array of ways they deal with these special days on the calendar. It may also mean that the widow doesn't want anything but that she knows her kids would like things done a certain way to help them. By the way, this applies to other family members, as well.

Afterword

I hope that *Facing Cancer as a Friend* has given you some insight into what life is like with cancer, as well as a wealth of ideas for supporting the person or people in your life as they face cancer with grace. If it has, please review this book.

Like other authors, I depend on reviews and recommendations to spread the word about my books. If Facing Cancer as a Friend has helped you in any way, please consider leaving a 5 star review on Amazon.com and on Goodreads. Also, share it on your favorite social media account. Thank you!

Also, check out my websites:

www.facingcancerwithgrace.com
www.heatherericksonauthor.com

I would love to hear from you! Let me know if you have any thoughts on *Facing Cancer as a Friend*. Was there anything I missed? Do you have any questions? Feel free to write to me at *heatherericksonauthor@gmail.com*.

Acknowledgments

I would first like to thank the Lord for giving me my husband, Dan, and the grace to face his cancer. I couldn't have asked for a better husband. I am grateful to have had Dan's unwavering love and support. He loved me well.

I am so thankful for each of **our children** who encourage me and bring their own brand of laughter and life to our home. I couldn't be prouder of you.

I am thankful for 3 particular support organizations that have made a tremendous difference in our ability to live well in spite of cancer and loss.

The Angel Foundation is a non-profit which supports families living with cancer in Minnesota. Our children gained grew more resilient through the years as they received support from the Angel Foundation and its volunteers.

Jack's Caregiver Coalition is a non-profit which supports men who are caregivers of cancer patients. While I am not a man, I facilitated their monthly Caregiver Klatch. The Klatch is Jack's version of a support group and is their only co-ed program.

Gilda's Club Twin Cities is a place for cancer patients and their caregivers and children to take classes, get support, and grow in the midst of cancer. Their Living with Loss group has been essential to my healing after the loss of my beloved husband, Dan.

Thank you to my **Advanced Reader Team** for your time, suggestions and support. You've made an incredible difference in the quality of this book.

I thank **my readers** who were so supportive of the first edition of Facing Cancer as a Friend. You were the inspiration for this second revised and updated edition.

Thank you to all of my **friends and family** who have been there for us in the good times and the hard places. Thank you for visits, meals, gifts, kind words and cards, help, and most of all, your prayers. God bless each of you, abundantly!

Other Books in the Facing Cancer Series

Facing Cancer as a Parent:
Helping your Children Cope with Your Cancer

Winner of the 2019 MIPA Award in the Health Category.

Also, check out

The Memory Maker's Journal:
Putting Your Memories into Words

Made in United States
Orlando, FL
04 August 2023